D1607342

ideas

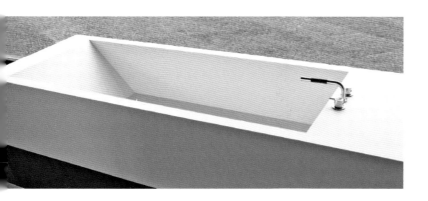

ideas

bathrooms
baños
salles de bains
badezimmer

AUTHORS
Fernando de Haro & Omar Fuentes

EDITORIAL DESIGN & PRODUCTION

EDITORES   PUBLISHERS

PROJECT MANAGERS
Carlos Herver Díaz
Ana Teresa Vázquez de la Mora
Laura Mijares Castellá

COORDINATION
Emily Keime López
Verónica Velasco Joos
Dulce Ma. Rodríguez Flores

PREPRESS COORDINATION
José Luis de la Rosa Meléndez

COPYWRITER
Víctor Hugo Martínez

ENGLISH TRANSLATION
Eva Dimitriadis

FRENCH TRANSLATION
Angloamericano de Cuernavaca - Carmen Chalamanch - Marta Pou

GERMAN TRANSLATION
Angloamericano de Cuernavaca - Sabine Klein

Ideas
bathrooms . baños . salles de bains . badezimmer

© 2012, Fernando de Haro & Omar Fuentes

AM Editores S.A. de C.V.
Paseo de Tamarindos 400 B, suite 102, Col. Bosques de las Lomas,
C.P. 05120, México, D.F., Tel. 52(55) 5258 0279
E-mail: ame@ameditores.com   www.ameditores.com

ISBN: 978-607-437-217-5

Printed in China.

INDEX • ÍNDICE

introduction • introducción • introduction • einleitung 8

introduction   introducción

Bathrooms are historically one of the places at homes where intimacy and beauty merge in space. They are also those places where recognition with the body, with oneself is reached through all the senses. They are, more than a service space, a place of recognition and comfort that has evolved over the past two centuries in a conclusive way since it is deeply linked to cultural conception of comfort in society.

Los cuartos de baño son históricamente uno de lo lugares del hogar donde la intimidad y la bellez se fusionan en el espacio. También son esos lugare donde se alcanza un reconocimiento con el cuerpo con uno mismo a través de todos los sentidos Son, más que un espacio de servicio, un lugar d reconocimiento y confort que ha evolucionad en los últimos dos siglos de manera contundent al encontrarse profundamente vinculado a l concepción cultural del confort en la sociedad.

introduction   einleitung

es salles de bain constituent, historiquement, un des ndroits de la maison où l'intimité et la beauté se lsionnent dans l'espace. Ce sont aussi des endroits ù l'on atteint une reconnaissance de son corps, de oi-même, à travers tous ses sens. Plus qu'un espace e service, c'est un endroit de reconnaissance et onfort, qui a évolué au cours des derniers siècles e façon marquante à force de se trouver lié à la onception de confort dans la société.

Badezimmer waren schon immer einer der Räume des Hauses in dem Intimität und Schönheit in einem Bereich veschmelzen. Es sind auch Orte, in denen man in Kontakt mit seinem Körper steht, mit einem selbst, durch all seinen Sinnen. Sie sind, mehr als ein funktioneller Bereich, ein Ort der Wiederkennung und Komfort, der sich, durch seine enge Bindung an kulturelle Konzepte des Komforts in der Gesellschaft, beständig weiterentwickelt hat.

It is known that the Palace of Versailles contained at least one hundred bathrooms. Only in the royal apartments, there were seven. These places were configured at that time with the presence of a bidet and two tubs, one for washing and one for rinsing. The initial conception of the toilet was excluded from that spatial configuration to be positioned discreetly in a confined space near the bedroom.

During the eighteenth and nineteenth century, hygiene was not a fundamental aspect of personal care. Nevertheless, this idea was consolidated a century later by the comfort level that represented the experience to be in a bathroom. Historical studies suggest that bathing was considered a pleasant way to spend time, rather than a necessity, and the bathrooms were seen as a fashion accessory, intended for taking a hot bath to relax and not as a necessary facility in the domestic environment. How else can we explain the frequency with which the existence of bathrooms is registered after being whimsically removed?

Se sabe que el Palacio de Versalles contenía por menos cien cuartos de baño; sólo en los apartamen reales había siete. Estos espacios se configurabo en ese tiempo con la presencia de un bidet y d bañeras, una para lavarse y otra para enjugarse. concepción inicial del inodoro quedaba excluic de esa configuración espacial para posicionar discretamente en un espacio confinado cerca al dormitorio.

Durante el Siglo XVIII y XIX la limpieza no era un aspec fundamental del cuidado personal; sin embargo e idea se fue consolidando un siglo después por el nivel comodidad que representaba vivir la experienc de encontrarse en una sala de baño. Estudios his ricos sugieren que el bañarse se consideraba u forma agradable de pasar el tiempo, en lugar una necesidad, y los cuartos de baño se percib como un accesorio de moda –por ejemplo, destir dos a darse un baño caliente para descansar-, y no u instalación necesaria dentro del ambiente domésti

n sait que le palais de Versailles avait au moins cent
les de bain; rien que dans les habitations royales,
en avait sept. Ces espaces étaient formés à cette
oque par la présence d'un bidet et de deux
ignoires, l'une pour se laver et l'autre pour se rincer.
conception initiale de WC était exclue de cette
nfiguration spatiale pour se situer discrètement dans
espace confiné près de la chambre à coucher.

ndant le XVIIIème et XIXème siècle, la propreté
tait pas un aspect fondamental des soins
rsonnels; cependant, cette idée fut consolidée
siècle plus tard par le niveau de confort que
résentait vivre l'expérience de se trouver dans
e salle de bain. Les recherches historiques sug-
rent que le bain était considéré comme une façon
réable de passer le temps, mais pas un besoin, et
salles debain étaient perçues comme un acces-
e à la mode, destinées, par exemple, à prendre un
n tiède pour se reposer, et non comme une
allation nécessaire dans un milieu domestique.

Es ist bekannt, dass das Schloss von Versailles
mindestens hundert Badezimmer hatte; allein in den
königlichen Räumen gab es sieben. Diese Bereiche
wiesen in dieser Zeit ein Bidet und zwei Badewannen
auf, eine um sich zu waschen und eine um sich
abzuspülen. Die ursprüngliche Version der Toilette
blieb aus diesem Konzept ausgeschlossen, um diskret
in einem geschlossenen Bereich in der Nähe des
Schlafzimmers untergebracht zu werden.

Im 18. und 19. Jahrhundert war Sauberkeit kein
wichtiger Aspekt in der persönlichen Pflege; jedoch
wurde diese Idee ein Jahrhundert später durch die
Annehmlichkeiten, die das Erlebnis eines Badezimmers
mit sich bringt, etabliert. Studien der Geschichte
legen nahe, dass baden als ein angenehmer
Zeitvertreib betrachtet wurde und nicht als eine
Notwendigkeit, und Badezimmer als modisches
Accessoire gesehen wurden – zum Beispiel um ein
warmes Bad zum Ausruhen zu nehmen-, und nicht
als ein notwendiger Teil des häuslichen Ambiente.

Instead, the attention given for the supply of hot water and the elaborate decoration of these rooms, indicated that cleaning, or at least showering, was becoming more important in society.

The idea of comfort settled in the collective imagination and gradually this space intended for a privileged social class began to democratize finally reaching all social strata of our time. What bathroom represents nowadays besides cutting edge, is innovation in various ways: materials used as coatings, furniture that is no longer strictly functional, styles to configure the interior design, sophistication of architectural lighting and industrial design for each of the accessories that cause in a holistic manner a precise atmosphere for those who access these spaces. The charm to turn an everyday and routine moment into a ritual in the most intimate and subtle way.

¿Cómo, si no, explicar la frecuencia con la cual s registra la existencia de cuartos de baño que despué se eliminaban caprichosamente? En cambio, la ater ción que se dedicaba al suministro de agua calient y la complicada decoración de esas habitacione indicaba que la limpieza, o por lo menos el duchars iba adquiriendo más importancia entre la socieda

La idea de lo confortable se instaló en el imaginar colectivo y poco a poco este espacio destinado a ur clase social privilegiada comenzó a democratizar llegando por fin a todos los estratos sociales c nuestra época. Lo que en el baño representa ho en día además de vanguardia es innovación e diversos sentidos: en los materiales empleados com recubrimientos, en los muebles que han dejado c ser estrictamente funcionales, en los estilos pc configurar el diseño interior, en la sofisticación de iluminación arquitectónica y el diseño industrial c cada uno de los accesorios que provocan de mane holística una atmósfera precisa para quien accede estos espacios: el encanto de convertir un momer de cotidianidad y rutina en un ritual de la manera m intima y también la más sutil.

omment expliquer, autrement, la fréquence des salles
e bain, qui sont après capricieusement éliminés?
revanche, l'attention que l'on portait au débit d'eau
naude, et la décoration élaborée de ces pièces,
diquait que la propreté, ou du moins la douche,
enait de plus en plus d'importance dans la société.

dée du confort s'est installée dans l'imaginaire
ollectif, et peu à peu cet espace destiné à une classe
ciale privilégiée a commencé à se démocratiser,
rivant à toutes les couches sociales de notre
poque. Ce que la salle de bain représente de nos
urs, en plus d'une avant-garde, c'est une innovation
ans plusieurs sens : Matériaux employés comme
vêtement, les meubles qui ne sont plus strictement
nctionnels, les styles pour donner une forme au
esign d'intérieur, la sophistication de l'éclairage
chitectonique, et le design industriel de chacun
s accessoires qui provoquent de manière holistique
e ambiance précise pour celui qui entre dans ces
paces : le charme de transformer un moment de
otidienneté et routine en un rituel de la façon la
us intime ainsi que subtile.

Wie sollte man sonst die Häufigkeit erklären in der
Bäder zu finden waren, die später willkürlich entfernt
wurden? Die Aufmerksamkeit, die der Versorgung mit
warmen Wasser und der komplizierten Dekoration
dieser Räume gewidmet wurde, lässt hingegen darauf
schliessen, dass die Sauberkeit, oder wenigstens das
duschen, in der Gesellschaft immer wichtiger wurde.

Die Idee des Komforts wurde Teil der kollektiven Vor-
stellung und nach und nach wurde dieser, für eine
priveligierte gesellschaftliche Klasse gedachte, Bereich
demokratisiert bis er am Ende alle gesellschaftlichen
Schichten unserer Zeit erreicht hat. Heute repräsen-
tiert ein Bad, ausser Avantgarde, Neuheitliches
in verschiedenem Sinne: In den für die Verkleidungen
verwendeten Materialien, in den nicht mehr strikt
funtionellen Möbeln, in den Stilen, die die Dekoration
ausmachen, in der raffinierten Beleuchtung der
Architiktur und dem industriellen Design eines jeden
Elementes, die in ganzheitlicher Weise eine passende
Atmosphäre für den Benutzer dieser Räume bewirkt:
der Reiz einen alltäglichen und von Routine bestimmten
Augenblick in ein Ritual zu verwandeln, von grösster
Intimität und zugleich sehr subtil.

neutral
neutros
neutres
neutral

innovative
innovador
innovateur
innovativ

SING AUDACIOUSLY the presence of circular elements to host the
ower or the washbasins can provide a dynamic space. Combining
e warmth of wood in light tones with the opacity in green of the
viding elements helps privacy to be a controlled option without
sing the subtle atmosphere of the different sources of light that are
egrated in it.

CURRIR CON AUDACIA a la presencia de elementos circulares
ara albergar la ducha o los lavabos puede dotar de dinamismo
espacio. Combinar la calidez de la madera en tonos claros con
opacidad en verde de los elementos divisorios ayuda a que la
vacidad sea una opción controlada sin perder la atmósfera sutil
e propician las diferentes fuentes de luz que se integran en ella.

RECOURS AUDACIEUX à la présence d'éléments circulaires pour
ger la douche ou les lavabos peut doter de dynamisme un espace.
mbiner la chaleur du bois à tons clairs avec l'opacité du vert des
ments de division fait de l'atmosphère privée une option contrôlée,
s perdre l'ambiance subtile favorisée par les différentes sources
lumière qui s'y intègrent.

KÜHNE PRÄSENS von runden Elementen für die Dusche oder die
schbecken, kann einem Raum Dynamik verleihen. Das warme,
e Holz mit dem lichtundurchlässigen Grün der Trennelemente zu
nbinieren, hilft Privatheit zu einer kontrollierten Option zu machen,
e die subtile Atmosphäre, die die verschiedenen in ihr integrierten
tquellen spenden, zu verlieren.

In contrast to the smoothness of the main walls and accessories, some details incorporate texture and a color accent in a neutral range that privileges the whole space.

En contraste con la lisura de los muros principales y los accesorios, algunos detalles incorporan textura y un acento de color dentro de una gama neutra que privilegia el espacio en su conjunto.

En contraste avec la douceur des murs principaux et des accessoires, certains détails incorporent une texture et un accent de couleur dans une gamme neutre qui privilège l'espace dans son ensemble.

Kontrastierend zu der Glattheit der wichtigsten Wände und dem Zubehör, versehen einige Details den Raum mit Textur und Farbakzenten innerhalb eines neutralen Farbspektrums, die dem Bereich in seiner Gesamtheit zugute kommt.

The subtleness of interior design is based on the sobriety of the architectural line, which allows us to frame the landscape turning the shower area into a space of contemplation. An ideal setting to pamper two of our senses through water: touch and sight.

La sutileza del diseño interior se fundamenta en la sobriedad del trazo arquitectónico, el cual permite enmarcar el paisaje convirtiendo el área de ducha en un espacio de contemplación. Escenario ideal para consentir dos de nuestros sentidos a través del agua: el tacto y la vista.

La subtilité du design d'intérieur est fondée sur la sobriété du trait architectonique, qui permet d'encadrer le paysage en transformant l'espace de la douche en un lieu de contemplation. C'est une scène idéale pour gâter deux de nos sens à travers l'eau: le toucher et la vue.

Die Feinheit der Innendekoration basiert auf der Nüchternheit der architektonischen Linien, die die Landschaft einrahmen und den Bereich der Dusche in einen Ort der Beschaulichkeit verwandeln. Eine ideale Szenerie um zwei unserer Sinne durch das Wasser zu verwöhnen: den Tast- und den Sehsinn.verwöhnen: den Tast- und den Sehsinn.

minimalism   minimalismo   minimalisme   minimalismus

IT IS ESSENTIAL TO REVEAL THE IMPORTANCE OF EACH LINE in the design of a minimalist environment. Therefore, the color white is a must for expanding the visual boundaries of space and highlight perfection which means do without any decorative element. It will be possible to find beauty in the ethereal, in the presence of light or the charm of the sophisticated simplicity of the furniture, accessories, divisions or transitional spaces.

REVELAR LA IMPORTANCIA DE CADA LÍNEA es esencial en el diseño de un ambiente minimalista. Por ello, el color blanco es un referente obligado para expandir los límites visuales del espacio y resaltar el perfeccionamiento que significa prescindir de cualquier elemento ornamental. La belleza será posible encontrarla en lo etéreo, en la presencia de la luz o en el encanto de la sofisticada sencillez del mobiliario, los accesorios, las divisiones o los espacios de transición.

RÉVÉLER L'IMPORTANCE DE CHAQUE LIGNE est essentiel pour le design d'une ambiance minimaliste. C'est pour cela que la couleur blanche est un référent obligatoire pour amplifier les limites visuelles de l'espace et rehausser le perfectionnement qui signifie se passer de tout élément ornemental. On pourra trouver la beauté dans l'éthéré, dans la présence de la lumière ou le charme de la simplicité sophistiquée du mobilier, les accessoires, les divisions ou les espaces de transition.

DIE BEDEUTUNG JEDER EINZELNEN LINIE offenzulegen ist essenziell in einem minimalistischen Ambiente. Daher ist die weisse Farbe ein notwendiger Bezug um die optischen Beschränkungen des Bereiches zu erweitern und die Perfektion, die mit dem Verzicht auf jegliche Verzierung einhergeht, hervorzuheben. Schönheit kann im ätherischen gefunden werden, in der Präsenz des Lichts oder im Reiz der raffinierten Schlichtheit der Möbel, des Zubehörs, der Unterteilungen oder den Übergangsbereichen.

The elegance of a monochromatic environment can reach another level of refinement when a detail or an object that reflects the taste and personality of the user is highlighted with the presence of the color black. A distinguished visual finish without pretention is highly recommended.

La elegancia de un ambiente monocromático puede alcanzar otro nivel de refinamiento al acentuar con la presencia del color negro un detalle o un objeto que refleje el gusto y la personalidad del usuario, un remate visual distinguido y sin pretensión es muy recomendable.

L'élégance d'une ambiance monochrome peut atteindre un autre niveau de raffinement en accentuant par la présence de la couleur noire un détail ou un objet qui reflète la personnalité ou le goût de l'usager, un couronnement visuel distingué et sans prétentions est fort recommandable.

Die Eleganz eines einfarbigen Ambientes kann ein anderes Niveau der Raffinesse erreichen, in dem mit schwarzer Farbe ein Detail oder ein Objekt betont wird, das den Geschmack und die Persönlichkeit des Benutzers wiederspiegelt, ein feiner, anspruchsloser optischer Abschluss ist sehr zu empfehlen.

Using the transparency as well as the geometry of straight and simple lines allows us to appreciate the qualities of every construction design detail. You should be very careful not to place objects in excess that visually pollute the space. Using the same materials for the diving eleme accessories and shelves favors harmony as well as a refined simplicity that makes it easier to appreciate the space as a unit from which ever secondary element emerges and not as a sum of different parts.

Recurrir a la transparencia así como a la geometría de trazos rectos y sencillos permite que puedan apreciarse las cualidades de cada detalle constructivo del diseño. Se debe ser muy cuidadoso de no caer en excesos en la colocación de objetos que contaminen visualmente el espacio. Emplear los mismos materiales para los elementos divisorios, accesorios y repisas favorece la armonía así como una depurada simplicidad que facilita que el espacio pueda apreciarse como una unidad del cual surge cada componente secundario y no como una su de piezas distintas.

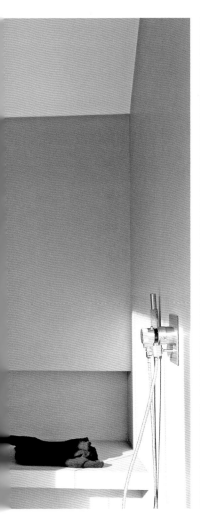

r recours à la transparence ainsi qu'à la géométrie de traits doits et simples permet d'apprécier les qualités de chaque détail constructif
lesign. On doit être très attentif pour ne pas tomber dans les excès en plaçant des objets qui contaminent visuellement l'espace. Employer
nêmes matériaux pour les éléments de division, les accessoires et les étagères favorise l'harmonie ainsi qu'une simplicité épurée par laquelle
ace peut être apprécié comme une unité dont surgit chaque composant secondaire, et non comme une somme de pièces différentes.

durchsichtige Flächen, sowie auf die Geometrie gerader und schlichter Linien zurückzugreifen, erlaubt die Eigenschaften eines jeden
chen Details des Designs zu schätzen. Man muss vorsichtig sein, nicht im Übermass Objekte aufzustellen, die den Bereich optisch
nreinigen. Für die Trennelemente, Accessoires und Regale das gleiche Material zu benutzen begünstigt Harmonie, sowie eine
Schlichtheit, die es einfacher macht den Bereich als eine Einheit zu betrachten, aus der jeder Bestandteil hervortritt, und nicht
ine Summe einzelner Stücke.

The use of the color sand that exhibits its different stone components generates an evocation of the elemental or rudimentary while being elegant. Not to include more than two color variations helps to maintain the neatness of the space.

El uso del color arena que exhibe sus diferentes componentes pétreos genera una evocación de lo elemental o lo rudimentario sin dejar de ser elegante. No incluir más de dos variaciones de color ayuda a conservar la pulcritud del espacio.

L'utilisation de la couleur sable qui exhibe ses différents composants de pierre génère une évocation de ce qui est élémentaire ou rudimentaire, tout en étant élégant. Ne pas inclure plus de deux variations aide à conserver la limpidité de l'espace.

Die Verwendung von Sandfarbe, die ihre verschiedenen Bestandte im Stein zeigt, erzeugt einen einfachen oder rudimentären Eindruc ohne seine Eleganz zu verlieren. Nicht mehr als zwei Farbvariante mit einzubeziehen hilft die Reinheit des Bereiches zu bewahren.

HOT TUB AND ACCESSORIES, washbasins or shower can the starring elements of the bathroom. Taking care that their ation in the space is suitable to go over them and contemplate m manages to make much more pleasant the experience when ng them. It is important that their lines correspond with each er and reflect the same language when what you are looking is to harmonize the environment.

JA TINA DE HIDROMASAJE así como sus accesorios, los abos o la regadera pueden ser los elementos protagó- os del baño. Cuidar que su ubicación sea idónea para orrerlos y también contemplarlos logra hacer la experiencia s amena al utilizarlos. Es importante que las líneas corres- ndan entre sí y reflejen un mismo lenguaje cuando se busca nonizar el ambiente.

UNE BAIGNOIRE POUR HYDROMASSAGE, ses accessoires, les lavabos ou la douche, peuvent être les éléments protagonistes de la salle de bain. Si on fait bien attention à leur disposition pour les parcourir et les contempler, leur utilisation sera une expérience plus appréciable. Il est important que leurs lignes se correspondent et reflètent un même langage quand on cherche à harmoniser l'ambiance.

EINE BADEWANNE MIT UNTERWASSERMASSAGE sowie die Armaturen oder die Dusche können Hauptelemente des Bades sein. Darauf zu achten, dass ihre Lage im Raum ideal ist um sie zu benutzen und auch zu betrachen, führt bei ihrer Benutzung zu einem sehr viel angenehmeren Erlebnis. Es ist wichtig, dass ihre Linien zueinander passen und die selbe Sprache wiederspiegeln, wenn man ein harmonisches Ambiente sucht.

THERE ARE ELEMENTS THAT ENRICH the concept of a bathroc with a neutral character. To incorporate a mat can provide textu and color caress; a large mirror expand the spatial dimension a increase the comfort level; an armchair ensure an atmosphere relaxation and comfort; a picture or various photographs in bla and white may be suitable for a unique visual finish.

EXISTEN ELEMENTOS QUE ENRIQUECEN el concepto de un ba con carácter neutro, incorporar un tapete puede brindar textura y u caricia de color; un gran espejo ampliar la dimensión espacic incrementar el grado de comodidad; un sillón procurar un ambie de relajación y confort; un cuadro o varias fotografías en blar y negro pueden ser idóneas para lograr un remate visual único.

IL Y A DES ÉLÉMENTS QUI ENRICHISSENT le concept d'une so de bain au caractère neutre ; ainsi, l'incorporation d'un tapis p donner une texture et une caresse de couleur; un grand miroir amplifier la dimension spatiale et augmenter la sensation de conf un fauteuil crée une ambiance de détente et de confort; une pein ou plusieurs photos en blanc et noir peuvent être parfaites p achever un couronnement visuel unique.

ES GIBT ELEMENTE, die ein Bad mit neutralem Charakter bereich einen Teppich beizufügen kann Textur und einen Hauch Fc spenden; ein grosser Spiegel die räumliche Grösse erweitern den Nutzen erhöhen; ein Sessel ein entspanntes und komforta Ambiente sichern; ein Gemälde oder einige Fotos in schwarz w können ideal für einen einzigartigen optischen Abschluss sein.

modern
moderno
moderne
modern

THE STONE COATINGS that have a discreet texture can b a very good choice to exalt the woodwork and the line of t bathroom furniture. It is recommended that lighting design h the same hue (color temperature) with the finishes to visuc represent a pleasant and comfortable to sight ambiance, withc contrasts of light.

LOS RECUBRIMIENTOS PÉTREOS que poseen una textu discreta pueden resultar una muy buena opción para enalted el trabajo de carpintería y la línea de los muebles de bar Es recomendable que el diseño de iluminación posea la mis tonalidad (temperatura de color) que los acabados para c visualmente represente un ambiente ameno y confortable la vista, sin contrastes lumínicos.

LES REVÊTEMENTS DE PIERRE à la texture discrète peuv constituer une excellente option pour faire ressortir menuiserie et la ligne des meubles de la salle de bain. Il recommandable que le design de l'éclairage ait une mê tonalité (température de la couleur) que les finitions, c que visuellement il représente une ambiance tranquille confortable à la vue, sans contrastes de luminosité.

DIE VERKLEIDUNGEN AUS STEIN, die eine diskrete Te aufweisen, können eine sehr gute Option sein, um Tischlerarbeiten und die Linien der Badezimmermöbel be zur Wirkung kommen zu lassen. Es ist zu empfehlen, dass Design der Beleuchtung die gleichen Töne (Temperatur der Fc verwendet werden, damit sich optisch ein ansprechendes angenehmes Bild, ohne Lichtkontraste, präsentiert.

For those who like to balance different design elements the eclectic style is an excellent choice. In it you can turn to for the visual accent of textures, colors and designer's accessories without the fear of being overloaded.

Para quienes gustan de equilibrar diferentes elementos de diseño el estilo ecléctico es una excelente opción. En él se puede recurrir al acento visual de las texturas, los colores y los accesorios de diseñador sin temor a resultar recargado.

Pour ceux qui aiment équilibrer différents éléments de design, le style éclectique est une excellente option. On peut y utiliser l'accent visuel des textures, les couleurs et les accessoires de design sans craindre que le résultat soit trop chargé.

Für alle, die verschiedene Designelemente in Gleichgewicht bringen wollen, ist der eklektische Stil eine hervorragende Option. In ihm kann kann auf die optischen Akzente der Texturen, Farben und Designerstücken zurückgreifen, ohne ein überladenes Ergebnis zu fürchten.

IT IS RECOMMENDED TO INCORPORATE more than two colors and different materials when looking for a contemporary character. Efforts should be made to define specific groups of elements that will have visual similarities such as color, texture or geometry. As a result, despite the diversity of individual characteristics the result will be enjoyable as a whole. A color tone can provide more personality.

INCORPORAR MÁS DE DOS COLORES y diferentes materiales es muy recomendable cuando se busca un carácter contemporáneo. Debe procurarse definir grupos específicos de elementos que tendrán similitudes visuales por ejemplo, su color, textura o geometría. Gracias a ello, a pesar de la diversidad de características particulares el resultado será agradable en su conjunto. Un acento de color puede darle más personalidad.

INCORPORER PLUS DE DEUX COULEURS et différents matériaux est très recommandable quand on cherche un caractère contemporain. On devrait définir des groupes spécifiques d'éléments ayant des similitudes visuelles, telles que leur couleur, leur texture ou leur géométrie. Grâce à cela, malgré la diversité des caractéristiques particulières, le résultat sera agréable dans son ensemble. Un accent de couleur peut lui donner un peu plus de personnalité.

MEHR ALS ZWEI FARBEN und verschiedene Materialien zu verwenden ist sehr zu empfehlen, wenn man einen zeitgemässen Charakter erreichen will. Man sollte darauf achten, die spezifischen Elemente nach optischen Ähnlichkeiten, zum Beispiel, in Farbe, Textur oder Geometrie in Gruppen zu definieren. Dann ist das Ergebnis in seiner Gesamtheit, trotz der Vielfalt der einzelnen Eigenschaften, angenehm. Ein Farbakzent verleiht mehr Persönlichkeit.

As glass is the predominant material it is possible to incorporate
wooden furniture in dark tones that allows observing its streaks.
The contrast between materials is pleasing to the eye.

Siendo el vidrio el material predominante existe la posibilidad de
incorporar mobiliario de madera en tonalidades oscuras que permitan
observar su veta, el contraste entre materiales resulta grato a la vista.

Quand le verre est le matériel dominant, on peut incorporer un
mobilier en bois à tonalités foncées qui permettent de voir sa veine,
et le contraste entre ces deux matériaux est agréable à la vue.

Obwohl Glas das vorherrschende Material ist, besteht die
Möglichkeit Möbel aus Holz in dunklen Tönen mit einer deutlichen
Maserung, zu verwenden; der Kontrast zwischen den Materialien ist
optisch angehm.

spaces of large amplitude you can use without problem the mbination of materials and textures. The design of the ceiling and or if sober, will allow a greater visual impact of the main spaces he bathroom.

espacios de gran amplitud puede recurrirse sin problema a la mbinación de materiales y texturas. El diseño del plafón y del o, si es sobrio permitirá un mayor impacto visual de los espacios cipales del baño.

Dans les espaces très amples, on peut utiliser sans aucun problème la combinaison de matériaux et textures. Si le design du plafond et du plancher est sobre, les espaces principaux de la salle de bain auront un impact plus grand.

In sehr grossen Räumen kann man ohne Probleme Materialien und Texturen kombinieren. Das Design der Decke und des Bodens erlaubt, wenn es schmucklos ist, eine grössere optische Wirkung der Hauptbereiche des Bades.

THE BEAUTY OF THE STONE is a peculiarity that may be exalted by using the faintest color it has on the walls of our bathroom. To make us of chrome taps with curved strokes will subtly reveal the beauty of a fresh and elegant atmosphere. To hide washbasins will provide visual neatness and privilege the architectural design of the space.

LA BELLEZA DE LA PIEDRA es una peculiaridad que puede ser enaltecida empleando el color más tenue que ésta posea en muros de nuestra sala de baño. Hacer uso de grifería cromada de trazos curvos revelará sutilmente la belleza de un ambiente fresco y elegante. Ocultar los lavabos otorgará limpieza visual y privilegiará el diseño arquitectónico en el que se encuentra

BEAUTÉ DE LA PIERRE est une particularité qui peut être rehaussée si l'on utilise sa couleur las plus douce pour les murs notre salle de bain. Une robinetterie chromée aux traits courbes révèlera avec subtilité la beauté d'une ambiance fraîche élégante. Les lavabos dissimulés donneront une propreté visuelle et privilégieront le design architectonique que les entoure.

SCHÖNHEIT DES STEINS ist eine Besonderheit, die noch erhöht werden kann, wenn man die hellste Farbe, die in ihm zu en ist, für die Wände des Bades benutzt. Verchromte Armaturen kurviger Formen zu verwenden, zeigt subtil die Schönheit s frischen und eleganten Ambientes. Die Waschbecken zu verbergen führt zu optischer Reinheit und stellt das architektonische gn, in dem sie sich befinden, heraus.

To make the shower look sophisticated and elegant, lies in emphasizing the geometry of the architecture generating a contrast between colors, shapes and the absence of textures. Sobriety dominates the environment.

Lograr que el área de ducha sea sofisticada y elegante, recae en enfatizar la geometría de la arquitectura generando un contraste entre colores, formas y la ausencia de texturas. La sobriedad domina el ambiente.

Pour obtenir un espace de douche sophistiqué et élégant, il faut souligner la géométrie de l'architecture en générant un contraste entre les couleurs, les formes et l'absence de textures. La sobriété domine l'ambiance.

Um zu erreichen, dass der Bereich der Dusche raffiniert und elegant wirkt, sollte die Geometrie der Architektur betont werden, einen Kontrast zwischen Farben und Formen schaffend und das Fehlen jeglicher Textur. Nüchternheit beherrscht das Ambiente.

rustic rústico rustique rustikal

THE CHARM OF THE RUSTIC focuses on proper selection of details and forms that can be conjugated to achieve spaces apparently simple but very comfortable. The ambient light and a color palette in light tones allow to highlight some constructive designs or original objects of handcrafted nature. Textures can never miss, they are unavoidably essential.

EL ENCANTO DE LO RÚSTICO se concentra en la selección adecuada de detalles y formas que pueden conjugarse para lograr espacios de aparente sencillez pero muy confortables. La luz ambiental y una paleta de color en tonalidades claras permiten destacar algunos diseños constructivos u objetos originales de carácter artesanal. Las texturas nunca pueden faltar, son inevitablemente esenciales.

LE CHARME DU RUSTIQUE se concentre dans le choix des détails et des formes qui peuvent se conjuguer pour réussir des espaces d'une simplicité apparente, mais très confortables. La lumière ambiance et une palette de couleurs aux tonalités claires permettent de souligner quelques designs constructifs ou des objets originaux à caractère artisanal. Les textures ne peuvent pas manquer, étant inévitablement essentielles.

DER REIZ DES RUSTIKALEN liegt in der angemessenen Wahl von Details und Formen, die zusammengefügt einen Bereich scheinbarer Einfachheit formen, aber sehr behaglich sind. Das Licht und eine Farbpalette in hellen Tönen erlaubt es, einige bauliche Details und originelle, kunsthandwerkliche Objekte hervorzuheben. Textur sollte nie fehlen, sie ist unverzichtbar.

Lines or irregular patterns provide a homey and neutral sensation. Color variations are minimum and finishes must demonstrate their constructive process. The result is a more human space where imperfection is part of beauty.

Los trazos o patrones irregulares otorgan una sensación hogareña y neutra. Las variaciones de color son mínimas y los acabados deben evidenciar su proceso constructivo. El resultado es un espacio más humano donde la imperfección es parte de la belleza.

Des traits ou des schémas irréguliers créent une sensation familière et neutre. Les variations de couleurs son minimales, et les finitions doivent mettre en évidence leur processus constructif. Le résultat est un espace plus humain où l'imperfection fait partie de la beauté.

Die unregelmässigen Linien und Muster erwecken einen heimeligen und neutralen Eindruck. Die Farbvarianten sind minimal und die Verarbeitung sollte immer den baulichen Prozess sichtbar lassen. Das Ergebnis ist ein menschlicherer Bereich, wo die Unvollkommenheit Teil der Schönheit ausmacht.

Decorating a rustic ambience should not be pretentious; on the contrary it should be casual, almost innocent. This is ideal for incorporating handcrafted objects of wicker or wood, including pots with plants or flowers in season or even a stony mat in light tones. The light should be diaphanous, preferably in warm colors and the location of objects and patterns or shapes on the walls can be random as long as it keeps similarity to other existing details or textures.

La decoración de un ambiente rústico no debe ser pretenciosa, por lo contrario debe ser casual, casi inocente. De este modo resulta id incorporar objetos artesanales de mimbre o madera; incluir macetas con plantas o flores de la estación o inclusive algún tapete pétreo matices claros. La luz debe ser diáfana, preferentemente en tonos cálidos y la ubicación de objetos así como de patrones o formas en muros puede ser aleatoria mientras mantenga similitud con otros detalles o texturas existentes.

écoration d'une ambiance rustique ne doit pas être prétentieuse, mais au contraire, informelle, presque innocente. Ainsi, l'idéal est
orporer des objets d'artisanat en osier ou en bois, inclure des pots avec des plantes ou des fleurs de la saison, et même un tapis de pierre
ons clairs. La lumière doit être limpide, de préférence à tons chauds, et la place des objets, ainsi que les schémas et les formes des murs,
être aléatoire, pourvu qu'elle garde une similitude avec les autres détails ou textures.

Dekoration eines rustikalen Ambiente darf nicht angeberisch sein, sie sollte im Gegenteil wie zufällig, fast unschuldig, wirken.
er sind kunsthandwerkliche Objekte aus Weiden oder Holz ideal; Pflanztöpfe mit Pflanzen oder Blumen der Jahreszeit oder sogar ein
ich aus Stein in hellen Farben. Das Licht sollte klar sein, bevorzugt in warmen Tönen und die Lage von Objekten sowie Mustern oder
en an den Wänden kann wie zufällig wirken, solange eine Ähnlichkeit mit anderen Details oder Texturen bewahrt wird.

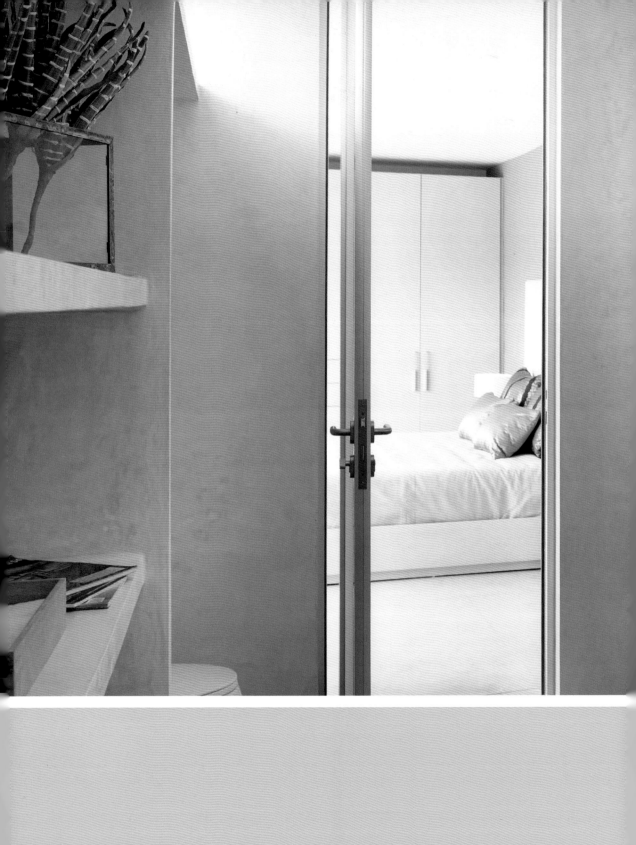

To rescue the vintage personality of an object and give those qualities to a space is fun and stylish. The elements incorporated in the decoration should be carefully chosen according to the dimensions of the space.

Rescatar la personalidad *vintage* de un objeto y darle esas cualidades a un espacio resulta divertido y elegante. Los elementos incorporados en la decoración deben ser cautelosamente seleccionados de acuerdo a las dimensiones del espacio.

Récupérer la personnalité *vintage* d'un objet et accorder cette qualité à un espace est amusant et élégant. Les éléments incorporés à la décoration doivent être méticuleusement choisis selon les dimensions de l'espace.

Den *Vintage* Aspekt eines Objektes zu retten oder diese Eigenschaft einem Bereich zu verleihen, ist amüsant und elegant. Die in der Dekoration verwendeten Elemente müssen vorsichtig, im Einklang mit den Ausmassen des Raumes, gewählt werden.

BEING THE TYPICAL COLORS OF THIS STYLE, beige, sand or grey it can be contrasted to all of them with darker wood furr

emphasizing the main area of the bathroom. The cushions and fabrics with discreet patterns will give you comfort and a plea

image to the entire environment in addition to a very cozy feeling reinforced by the reflection of vegetation and the ambient

SIENDO LOS COLORES TÍPICOS DE ESTE ESTILO, el beige, arena o gris, puede contrastarse a todos ellos con un mobi

en madera más oscura enfatizando el área principal del baño. Los almohadones y las telas con patrones discretos le c

comodidad y una placentera imagen a todo el ambiente además de un sentimiento muy acogedor reforzado por el refle

vegetación y la luz ambiental.

ANT QUE COULEURS TYPIQUES DE CE STYLE, le beige, le sable ou le gris peuvent être mis en contraste avec un
lier en bois plus foncé qui soulignera l'espace principal de la salle de bain. Les coussins et les tissus aux imprimés discrets
rteront du confort et une image agréable à toute m'ambiance, en plus d'un sentiment très accueillant renforcé par le reflet
végétation et la lumière ambiance.

IE TYPISCHEN FARBEN DIESES STILS Beige, Sandfarbe oder Grau ist, kann man sie durch eine Möblierung mit sehr
em Holz in Kontrast stellen und den Hauptbereich des Bades betonen. Die Kissen und Stoffe mit diskretem Muster spenden
emlichkeit und lassen, ausser ein gemütliches Gefühl, das durch die Spiegelungen der Pflanzen und des Lichts verstärkt
hervorzurufen, das gesamte Ambiente angenehm wirken.

The color ocher and the copper tones of the taps give a peculiar appearance to the space. If the walls have no texture, it is a great detail to incorporate it in the design of the floor, a niche or a bathtub.

El color ocre y los tonos cobrizos de la grifería dotan de una apariencia peculiar el espacio. Si los muros no tienen textura, resulta un excelente detalle incorporarla en el diseño del piso, de algún nicho o de la tina de baño.

La couleur ocre et les tons cuivrés de la robinetterie donnent une apparence particulière à l'espace. Si les murs n'ont aucune texture, un détail excellent est de l'incorporer au design du plancher, d'une niche ou une baignoire.

Die Ockerfarbe und die kupferfarbenen Armaturen geben dem Bereich ein besonderes Aussehen. Wenn die Wände keine Textur aufweisen ist es ein hervorragendes Detail, Textur im Design des Bodens, einer Nische oder der Badewanne einzuführen.

warm·cálidos
chaudes·warme

innovative
innovador
innovateur
innovativ

VERITABLE TREAT for the touch is to have various textures at
erent scales conducive to a true shower experience. The
ge of colors between materials and the contemplation of
landscape do the rest.

VERDADERO OBSEQUIO para el tacto es contar con
ersas texturas a diferentes escalas que propicien una
dadera experiencia al ducharse. La gama de colores entre
eriales y la contemplación del paisaje hacen el resto.

POUR LE TOUCHER, c'est un vrai cadeau que de disposer
de plusieurs textures à différentes échelles qui favorisent
une véritable expérience au moment de la douche. La gamme
de couleurs entre les matériaux et la contemplation du paysage
font le reste.

EIN WAHRES GESCHENK für den Tastsinn sind verschiedenste
Texturen in unterschiedlichen Ebenen, die aus dem Duschen
ein wirkliches Erlebnis machen. Die Farbpalette der Materialien und die Aussicht sorgen für den Rest.

The reddish wood tones together with chrome hardware, decorative pieces or stones in color white give a tranquil setting: reflection of elegance and solemnity.

Los tonos rojizos de la madera en conjunto con herrajes cromados, piezas decorativas o piedras en color blanco propician un ambiente sereno: reflejo de elegancia y solemnidad.

Les tons roux du bois unis aux garnitures chromées, des pièces décoratives ou des pierres en couleur blanche favorisent une ambiance de sérénité, reflet d'élégance et solennité.

Die rötlichen Töne des Holzes, zusammen mit den Chrombeschlägen, Dekorationsstücken oder dem weissen Stein, schaffen ein beschauliches Ambiente: ein Abglanz von Eleganz und Festlichke

PROPERLY SELECTING THE REQUIRED TYPE OF LIGHTING is essential to balance the space with light and harmonize i
the coatings having minimum color variation. To hide light in order to produce indirectly luminous areas will allow the bath
to have a higher degree of privacy and not saturate with shapes that are in our visual field. The presence of onyx for
support accessories is highly recommended.

SELECCIONAR ADECUADAMENTE EL TIPO DE ILUMINACIÓN requerida es indispensable para equilibrar de luz el espo
armonizarlo con los recubrimientos que posean una mínima variación de color. Ocultar las luminarias para producir indirecta
zonas luminosas permitirá que la sala de baaño posea un grado de intimidad mayor y no se sature de formas que se encu
en nuestro campo visual. La presencia de ónix para algunos accesorios de apoyo es muy recomendable.

INDISPENSABLE DE CHOISIR LE TYPE D'ÉCLAIRAGE APPROPRIÉ pour équilibrer la lumière de l'espace et l'harmoniser
les revêtements qui possèdent une légère variation de couleur. Dissimuler les sources de lumière pour produire indirectement
ones lumineuses permettra que la salle de bain ait un plus haut degré d'intimité et ne se sature pas des formes qui se
ent dans notre champ visuel. La présence d'onyx pour certains accessoires d'appui est fort recommandable.

ENÖTIGTE BELEUCHTUNG ANGEMESSEN ZU WÄHLEN, ist unabdinglich, um den Bereich gleichmässig mit Licht zu
gen und ihn mit den Verkleidungen in minimalen Farbvarianten in Harmonie zu bringen. Die Leuchten zu verdecken, um
he mit indirektem Licht zu schaffen, erlaubt dem Bad eine grössere Intimität zu haben und es nicht mit den Formen, die
n unserem Sichtfeld befinden, zu übersättigeen. Die Verwendung von Onyx in einigen Assessoires ist sehr zu empfehlen.

MINIMALISM has been enriched with the passing of time: beyond the use of the color white to show purity and the value of the design of the essential, the color has begun to take a more relevant role in the universe of lines of geometric simplicity. Today is viable to combine various elements as long as it keeps the golden rule: not to fall into decorative excesses.

EL MINIMALISMO se ha enriquecido con el paso del tiempo: más allá del empleo del color blanco para manifestar pureza y el valor del diseño de lo esencial, el color ha comenzado a tomar un rol más relevante dentro del universo de los trazos de simplicidad geométrica. Hoy es viable combinar elementos distintos siempre y cuando se cumpla la regla de oro: no caer en desbordes decorativos.

LE MINIMALISME s'est enrichi avec le temps: au-delà de l'utilisation de la couleur blanche pour manifester la pureté et la valeur du design de l'essentiel, la couleur a commencé à jouer un rôle plus important dans l'univers des traits de simplicité géométrique. Il est possible aujourd'hui de combiner des éléments différents à condition de respecter la règle d'or: ne pas tomber dans les débordements décoratifs.

DER MINIMALISMUS wurde im Laufe der Zeit bereichert: über die Verwendung von weisser Farbe, um Reinheit auszudrücken und dem Wert des Designs des Unverzichtbaren hinaus, beginnt die Farbe eine wichtigere Rolle im Universum der Linien schlichter Geometrie zu spielen. Heute ist es möglich verschiedene Elemente zu kombinieren, solange die goldene Regel beachtet wird: nicht in eine übertriebene Dekoration zu verfallen.

minimalism
minimalismo
minimalisme
minimalismus

Considering that all the objects have a role to play, find them a place
to stand out and almost become sculptural pieces gives excellent
results in free spaces of ornamentation.

Tomando en cuenta que todos los objetos tienen una función que
cumplir, encontrarles un lugar para que resalten y casi se conviertan
en piezas escultóricas da excelentes resultados en espacios libres
de ornamentación.

Prenant en compte que tous les objets ont une fonction à remplir,
leur trouver un endroit qui les mette en valeur et les transforme presque
en sculptures donne d'excellents résultats dans les espaces libres
d'ornements.

Beachtend, dass alle Objekte eine Funktion zu erfüllen haben, ist
einen Platz für sie zu finden in dem sie zur Geltung kommen und sich
fast in Skulpturen verwandeln, eine hervorragende Lösund in Räumen
die frei von jeglichem Schmuck sind.

RTING FROM A BASE IN COLOR WHITE, carpentry can stand
pleasantly. Birch wood lets us appreciate a dim contrast that
ofs that in this style the quality of the unions and the details
ermine to a large extent the quality of the designed space.

TIENDO DE UNA BASE EN COLOR BLANCO, el trabajo
carpintería puede hacerse destacar gratamente. Madera
10 el Abedul permite que se aprecie un atenuado contraste
evidencia que en este estilo la calidad de las uniones
s detalles determina en gran medida la calidad del espa-
diseñado.

PARTANT D'UNE BASE EN COULEUR BLANCHE, on peut
re en relief agréablement le travail de menuiserie. Le bois
jue le bouleau permet d'apprécier un contraste atténué qui
en évidence que dans ce style la qualité des unions et des
ils définit en grande partie la qualité de l'espace créé par
esign.

GEHEND VON EINER BASIS IN WEISS, können die
lerarbeiten angenehm herausgestellt werden. Holz, wie Birke,
bt einen sanften Kontrast zu würdigen, der beweist, dass
esem Stil die Qualität der Verbindungen und der Details in
em Ausmass die Qualität des Bereiches bestimmt.

modern
moderno
moderne
modern

WHEN WE TALK ABOUT ARCHITECTURE not everything is conceived in straight lines or thought as a white canvas impossible to touch, exclusive for contemplation. The features that are integrated in the interior design narrate our personality and taste, turn to them through colors, shapes, textures or lighting systems may involve original variations to the most common objects of these spaces, such as mirrors.

CUANDO DE ARQUITECTURA SE HABLA no todo puede concebirse en trazos rectos ni pensarse como un lienzo en blanco imposible de tocar, exclusivo para la contemplación. Las particularidades que se integran en el diseño interior narran nuestra personalidad y gusto, recurrir a ellas a través de colores, formas, texturas o sistemas de iluminación pueden implicar variantes novedosas a los objetos mas comunes de estos espacios, por ejemplo los espejos.

QUAND ON PARLE D'ARCHITECTURE, on ne peut pas tout concevoir en traits droits ni penser comme une toile vierge intouchable, réservée à la contemplation. Les particularités qui sont intégrées dans le design d'intérieurs racontent notre personnalité et notre goût, s'en servir à travers les couleurs, les formes, les textures ou les systèmes d'éclairage peut impliquer des variantes pleines de nouveauté pour les objets les plus communs dans ces espaces, comme les miroirs, par exemple.

WENN MAN ÜBER ARCHITEKTUR SPRICHT, kann man weder alles als gerade Linien empfinden, noch als eine weisse Leinwand die man nicht anfassen darf, nur zum Betrachten gedacht. Die Eigenarten, die das Innendesign umschliesst, erzählen von unserer Persönlichkeit und unserem Geschmack; auf sie durch die Farben, Formen, Texturen und Beleuchtung zurückzugreifen, kann den alltäglichsten Objekten dieses Bereiches, zum Beispiel den Spiegeln, neuartige Varianten verleihen.

THE ARCHITECTURAL DETAILS or those formal gestures made with innovative materials should not lose their quality of fra the space. They should not distract, they should lead to the understanding of the entire set, whose essence necessarily be to the interior space.

LOS DETALLES ARQUITECTÓNICOS o aquellos gestos formales realizados con materiales novedosos no deben de perc cualidad de enmarcar el espacio. No deben de distraer, deben de conducir a la comprensión de todo el conjunto, a cuya es necesariamente pertenecen en el espacio interior.

DÉTAILS D'ARCHITECTURE ou les gestes formels achevés avec des matériaux nouveaux ne doivent pas perdre leur qualité cadrement pour l'espace. Ils ne doivent pas distraire, mais conduire à la compréhension de l'ensemble, à l'essence duquel partiennent nécessairement dans l'espace extérieur.

RCHITEKTONISCHEN DETAILS oder jene formalen Gesten aus neuartigen Materialien, dürfen beim Umrahmen des Raumes ihre Qualitäten verlieren. Sie dürfen nicht ablenken, sollten zum Verständnis des Ganzen führen, zu deren Essenz sie im bereich notwendigerweise gehören.

Order is a cardinal point in modern style. To give the ideal space to each object favors our sense of sight to be relaxed and able to perceive every construction detail or the design of the furniture, which causes pleasant emotions.

El orden es un eje cardinal dentro del estilo moderno. Dar el espacio ideal a cada objeto favorece que nuestro sentido de la vista se encuentre relajado y susceptible de percibir cada detalle capaz de provocarnos emociones.

L'ordre est un axe cardinal dans le style moderne. Si chaque objet est placé dans son espace idéal, notre sens de la vue est détendu et susceptible de percevoir chaque détail constructif, ou le design du mobilier, pour nous provoquer des émotions agréables.

Ordnung ist eine Hauptachse im modern Stil. Jedem Objekt seinen idealen Platz zu geben, erleichtert es unserem Sehsinn sich zu entspannen und so jedes bauliche Detail oder das Design der Möbel zu bemerken, um uns angenehm zu fühlen.

REFLECTIONS in addition of causing an amplification of space can help us discover symmetrical compositions that generate lightness, fragility or continuity. To achieve this we can use floor to ceiling mirrors and horizontal stripes illuminated from the back. Covers suspended from the washbasins or the presence of ornamental elements such as vegetation visibly enrich when the space is not so big.

LOS REFLEJOS además de provocar una amplificación del espacio pueden ayudarnos a descubrir composiciones simétricas que generen ligereza, fragilidad o continuidad. Para lograrlo se puede recurrir a espejos de piso a techo y franjas horizontales iluminadas desde la parte posterior. Las cubiertas suspendidas de los lavabos o la presencia de elementos de ornato como la vegetación enriquecen visiblemente cuando el espacio no es tan grande.

LES REFLETS provoquent non seulement une amplification de l'espace, mais peuvent nous aider aussi à découvrir des compositions symétriques qui génèrent légèreté, fragilité ou continuité. Pour ceci, on peut utiliser des miroirs du toit auplancher et des franges horizontales avec un éclairage postérieur. Les bases suspendues pour lavabo ou la présence d'ornements tels que la végétation enrichissent visiblement lorsque l'espace n'est pas si grand.

SPIEGELUNGEN, davon abgesehen, dass sie den Raum vergrössern, können dabei helfen symmetrische Kompositionen zu entdecken, die Leichtigkeit, Zerbrechlichkeit oder Kontinuität erzeugen. Um das zu erreichen, kann man Spiegel von Boden bis zur Decke verwenden und horizontale von hinten beleuchtete Flächen. Die hängenden Abdeckungen der Waschbecken oder die Schmuckstücke, wie die Pflanzen, bereichern optisch, wenn der Bereich nicht sehr gross ist.

There are not written rules to conceive space. It can be dynamic and sensual; provocative and lively; different and elegant. A bathroom should be a sensory haven for the user at all times.

No hay reglas escritas para concebir un espacio. Se puede ser dinámico y sensual; provocativo y alegre; diverso y elegante. Una sala de baño debe ser un refugio sensorial para el usuario en todo momento.

Il n'y a pas de règles écrites pour concevoir un espace. On peut ê dynamique et sensuel, provocateur et joyeux, divers et élégant. Un salle de bain doit être à tout moment un refuge sensoriel pour l'usc

Es gibt keine geschriebenen Regeln wie ein Bereich zu entwerfen Er kann dynamisch und sinnlich sein; provozierend und fröhlich; a wechslungsreich und elegant. Ein Badezimmer sollte für den Benut zu jeder Zeit ein sinnlicher Zufluchtsort sein.

There always exists the possibility to include a designer's piece that is part of our favorite objects. The hallmark may be its color preferably strong or its shape of organic qualities.

Siempre puede existir la posibilidad de incluir una pieza de diseñador que sea parte de nuestros objetos favoritos. El sello distintivo puede ser su color preferentemente encendido o su forma de cualidades orgánicas.

Il est toujours possible d'inclure une pièce design qui fasse partie de nos objets préférés. Le sceau distinctif peut en être la couleur, de préférence vive, ou sa forme de qualités organiques.

Es gibt immer die Möglichkeit ein Designerstück zu verwenden, das einer unserer Lieblingsstücke ist. Sein besonderes Merkmal kann seine Farbe sein, am liebsten kräftig, oder seine Form von organischer Qualität.

rustic
rústico
rustique
rustikal

THE PRESENCE OF UNIQUE OBJECTS placed with apparent indifference in warm atmospheres favors to evoke the passing of time and the rustic character of the design. The wood must preserve its appearance or color while the walls must convey a sense of smoothness provoking the touch.

LA PRESENCIA DE OBJETOS SINGULARES colocados con aparente indiferencia dentro de atmosferas cálidas favorece a evocar el paso del tiempo y el carácter rústico del diseño. La madera debe conservar su apariencia o color mientras que los muros deben de trasmitir una sensación de lisura provocando el tacto.

LA PRÉSENCE D'OBJETS SINGULIERS placés avec une indifférence apparente dans les ambiances accueillantes favorise l'évocation du temps qui passe et le caractère rustique du design. Le bois doit conserver son apparence ou sa couleur, tandis que les murs doivent transmettre une sensation de douceur qui attire le toucher.

DIE PRÄSENZ EINZIGARTIGER OBJEKTE, die scheinbar wahllos in warmen Atmosphären aufgestellt sind, erleichtert es das Vergehen der Zeit und den rustikalen Charakter des Designs heraufzubeschwören. Das Holz sollte sein Aussehen oder seine Farbe behalten, während die Wände ein Gefühl von Glattheit vermitteln sollten, die den Tastsinn provoziert.

To use a handcrafted frame finely crafted is an excellent complement to highlight a detail on a small scale. The combination of tones may be balanced without any problem with a maximum of three colors.

Recurrir a un marco de manufactura artesanal finamente trabajado es un excelente complemento para resaltar un detalle de pequeña escala. La combinación de tonalidades puede equilibrarse sin ningún problema con un máximo de tres colores.

Un cadre de manufacture artisanale finement travaillé est un excellent complément pour mettre en valeur un détail à petite échelle. La combinaison de tonalités peut être équilibrée sans problème avec un maximum de trois couleurs.

Auf einen feinen handgearbeiteten Rahmen zurückzugreifen ist eine hervorragende Ergänzung, um ein kleines Detail herauszustellen. Die Kombination der Farbtöne kann ohne Problem mit einem Maximum von drei Farben ausgeglichen werden.

THE TONE MATTE OF THE WALL AND ITS CLARITY are the ideal background to notice the ancient and rudimentary nature of the mirror frame or the base for the washbasin. Everything makes sense when we observe closely that each piece seems to have been made by hand in a slow manufacturing process. Visually, surfaces should be opposing between furniture, walls and floors. The cutting lines of each piece of wood, imperceptible and charming.

EL TONO MATE DE LA PARED Y SU CLARIDAD son el fondo ideal para hacer notar la naturaleza antigua y rudimentaria del marco en el espejo o la base para el lavabo. Todo cobra sentido al observar detalladamente que cada pieza parece haber sido realizada a mano en un lento proceso de fabricación. Visualmente las superficies deben ser opuestas entre mobiliario, muros y pisos. Las líneas de corte de cada pieza de madera imperceptibles y encantadoras.

LE TON MAT DU MUR ET SA CLARTÉ constituent le fond idéal pour faire valoir la nature ancienne et rudimentaire du cadre dans le miroir et la base pour lavabo. Tout prend sens quand on observe au détail que chaque pièce semble avoir été faite à la main dans un lent processus de fabrication. Visuellement, les surfaces doivent être opposées entre le mobilier, les murs et les planchers, les hachures de chaque pièce imperceptibles et charmantes.

DER MATTE TON DER WAND UND IHRE HELLIGKEIT sind er ideale Hintergrund um die antike und einfache Natur des Spiegelrahmes oder die Basis des Waschbeckens zu betonen. Alles macht Sinn, wenn man im Detail bemerkt, dass alle Stücke in einem langsamen Prozess handgearbeitet zu sein scheinen. Optisch sollten die Oberflächen Gegensätze zu den Möbeln, Wänden und Böden sein. Die Schnittlinien jedes Holzstückes sind unauffällig und bezaubernd.

intense
intensos
intenses
intensiv

INTENSITY can be described as the amount of stimuli our body receives through certain physical components that produce visual or spatial resonance by means of color, the diversity of geometrical figures or light that combine in a bathroom environment. Audacity and creativity are the two components that must be kept in mind when merging languages: the day-to-day, the ordinary can reveal a new timeless beauty.

LA INTENSIDAD puede describirse como la cantidad de estímulos que nuestro cuerpo recibe por medio de ciertos componentes físicos que producen resonancia visual o espacial por medio del color, la diversidad de formas geométricas o de luz que se conjuguen en un ambiente de baño. Audacia y creatividad son el par de componentes que debe tenerse en mente al momento de fusionar lenguajes: lo cotidiano, lo común puede revelar una nueva belleza atemporal.

L'INTENSITÉ peut être décrite comme la quantité de stimuli que reçoit notre corps au moyen de certains composants physiques qui produisent une résonnance visuelle ou spatiale au moyen de la couleur, la diversité de formes géométriques ou de lumière qui se conjuguent dans l'ambiance d'une salle de bain. Audace et créativité sont les deux composants qu'on doit avoir en tête au moment de fusionner les langages: le quotidien, le commun, peut révéler une nouvelle beauté intemporelle.

INTENSITÄT kann man als die Summe der Reize beschreiben, die unser Körper empfängt, die, durch die im Ambiente des Badezimmers zusammentreffenden Farben, die Vielfalt an geometrischen Formen oder des Lichts, eine optische oder räumliche Resonanz produzieren. Kühnheit und Kreativität sind die zwei Komponenten, die man im Moment verschiedene Stile miteinander zu verbinden, beachten sollte: Alltägliches, das Gewöhnliche kann eine neue, zeitlose Schönheit offenbaren.

innovative
innovador
innovateur
innovativ

geometric patterns of coatings should have a similarity with the
ure used. For the selection of light fixtures we should monitor
hese integrate with decorative elements such as paintings
corative vases. There is no restriction in the saturation of
ents with texture or color difference.

atrones geométricos de los recubrimientos deben tener una
ud con el mobiliario empleado. En el caso de la selección de
arias debe vigilarse que éstas dialoguen con elementos
ativos como pinturas o jarrones decorativos. No hay restricción
saturación de elementos con textura o diferencia de color.

Les schémas géométriques des revêtements doivent avoir une similitude
avec le mobilier. Dans le cas du choix des sources de lumière, on doit
faire en sorte qu'elles dialoguent avec les éléments décoratifs, tels
que les peintures ou les vases. Il n'y a aucune restriction quant à la
saturation d'éléments à textures ou couleurs différentes.

Die geometrischen Formen der Verkleidungen sollten dem verwendeten
Mobiliar ähneln. Bei den gewählten Lampen sollte man prüfen, ob sie
mit den dekorativen Elementen, wie Farben oder dekorativen Krügen
einhergehen. Es gibt keinerlei Beschränkungen im Sättigungsgrad der
Elemente mit Texturen oder verschiedenen Farben.

To consider that the bathtub is besides a functional object, furniture for relaxation turns out to be immensely enjoyable that its position has a privileged view of the environment.

Al considerar que la tina de baño es además de un objeto funcional un mueble para el descanso, resulta inmensamente agradable que su posición tenga una vista privilegiada del entorno.

Si l'on considère que la baignoire est en plus d'un objet fonctionnel, un meuble pour le repos, il est extrêmement agréable que sa position ait une vue privilégiée sur son entourage.

Wenn man bedenkt, dass die Badewanne nicht nur ein funktionelles Objekt ist, sondern auch der Entspannung dient, erweist es sich als sehr angenehm, dass ihre Position eine privilegierte Sicht auf die Umgebung erlaubt.

THE RELATIONSHIP BETWEEN INTERIOR AND EXTERIOR that large windows favor can be emphasized through a bold lighting design that can be transformed throughout the day. The resting place of perhaps the greatest privilege should be the bathtub. It is the most important piece to fully pamper our five senses. It is recommended not to use curtains.

LA RELACIÓN ENTRE INTERIOR Y EXTERIOR que propician los grandes ventanales puede subrayarse por medio de un diseño de iluminación audaz que a lo largo del día pueda irse transformando. El lugar de descanso y quizá el de mayor privilegio debe ser la tina de baño, es la pieza más importante para consentir a plenitud nuestros cinco sentidos. Recomendable no hacer uso de cortinas.

LA RELATION ENTRE L'INTÉRIEUR ET L'EXTÉRIEUR favorisé par les grandes fenêtres peut être rehaussé par un design d'éclairage audacieux, qui se transformera au long de la journée. Le lieu de repos, et peut-être le plus privilégié, doit être la baignoire, qui est la pièce la plus importante pour gâter pleinement nos cinq sens. On recommande de se passer de rideaux.

DIE VERBINDUNG ZWISCHEN INNEN- UND AUSSENBEREICH, die die grossen Wandfenster herstellen, kann man mit einer kühnen Beleuchtung unterstreichen, die sich im Laufe des Tages verändert. Ein Ort der Ruhe und vielleicht der privilegierteste Platz sollte die Badewanne sein, sie ist das wichtigste Stück um unsere fünf Sinne nach Kräften zu verwöhnen. Man sollte auf Vorhänge verzichten.

Including the repetition of visual elements in upholstery can help reduce the far-fetched of some furniture without taking away prominence. To achieve a vintage environment we should consider the shades of color and the design of taps.

Incluir la repetición de elementos visuales en tapices puede ayudar a disminuir lo rebuscado de algunos muebles sin quitarles protagonismo. Para lograr un ambiente de época deben cuidarse las tonalidades del color y el diseño de la grifería.

Inclure la répétition d'éléments visuels dans les teintures peut aider à atténuer l'aspect recherché de certains meubles, sans les priver de leur rôle de protagonistes. Pour réussir une ambiance d'époque, on doit soigner les tonalités de couleur et le design de la robinetterie.

Die Wiederholung von optischen Elementen auf der Tapete hilft das Gekünstelte einiger Möbel abzuschwächen, ohne ihnen die Hauptrolle zu nehmen. Um ein zeitgemässes Ambiente zu erzielen, sollte auf die Farbtöne und das Design der Armaturen geachtet werden.

USE AS A BASE COLOR BLACK gives us the opportunity to
Jde a radical change of textures and shades to enhance the
gn of some light fixtures that can evoke marine life. The circular
or or the appearance of the vibrant finishings that can show
nimsical distribution almost handcrafted.

ZAR COMO BASE EL COLOR NEGRO nos da la oportunidad
Jcluir un cambio radical de texturas y matices para resaltar el
ĩo de algunas luminarias que pueden evocar la vida marina;
spejo en forma circular o la apariencia de los acabados
Jntes que puede aparentar una distribución caprichosa
artesanal.

ISATION DU NOIR COMME COULEUR DE BASE nous offre
Jssibilité d'introduire un changement radical de textures et
Jances afin de faire ressortir le design de certaines lampes
euvent évoquer la vie maritime; le miroir de forme circulaire
Ispect des finitions vibrantes peut donner l'apparence d'une
Jution capricieuse, presque artisanale.

WARZ ALS GRUNDFARBE ZU WÄHLEN, gibt uns die Mög-
it einen radikalen Wechsel der Texturen und Schattierungen
suchen, um das Design einiger Leuchten hervorzuheben, die
eben im Meer heraufbeschwören; der runde Spiegel oder
aftvolle Wand, die wie eine eigenwillige, fast künstlerische,
nung wirkt.

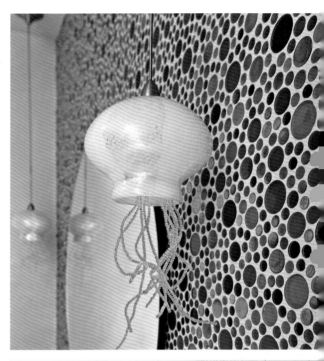

IN MINIMALIST ENVIRONMENTS the presence of dualities shouldn't be neglected: black and white set an ideal atmosphere to highlight the perfection of the design. Reflexes or framework on polished surfaces cause a sense of softness and neatness.

EN LOS AMBIENTES MINIMALISTAS no debe dejarse de lado la presencia de dualidades: el blanco y negro configuran una atmósfera ideal para destacar el perfeccionamiento del diseño. Los reflejos o entramados en las superficies pulidas provocan una sensación de suavidad y pulcritud.

DANS LES AMBIANCES MINIMALISTES, on ne doit pas laisser de côté la présence de dualités: le blanc et le noir créent une atmosphère idéale pour faire ressortir le perfectionnement du design. Les reflets ou entrecroisements sur les surfaces polies provoquent une sensation de douceur et propreté.

IN EINEM MINIMALISTISCHEN AMBIENTE sollte man nicht auf die Präsenz von Dualität verzichten: Schwarz und Weiss schaffen eine ideale Atmosphäre, um die Perfektion des Designs herauszustellen. Die Spiegelungen oder Verpflechtungen auf den glänzenden Oberflächen lassen den Eindruck von Sanftheit und Reinheit entstehen.

minimalism
minimalismo
minimalisme
minimalismus

Having an open dressing room to project variations of colors and textures can cause a certain degree of saturation, however if within the same space we use a large element of brightly lit color the appearance will be harmonious and at the same time elegant.

Contar con un vestidor abierto que proyecte variaciones de colores y texturas puede causar cierto grado de saturación, sin embargo si dentro del mismo espacio empleamos un gran elemento de color muy bien iluminado, la apariencia será armónica sin dejar de ser elegante.

Un vestiaire ouvert qui projette des variations de couleurs et de textures peut provoquer un certain degré de saturation, mais si à l'intérieur de ce même espace nous utilisons un grand élément de couleur très bien éclairé, l'apparence sera harmonieuse, ainsi qu'élégante.

Einen offenen Ankleideraum zu haben, der eine Variante an Farben und Texturen ausstrahlt, kann eine gewisse Sättigung verursachen, zweifelsohne wirkt er harmonisch, ohne seine Eleganz zu verlieren, wenn sich in ihm ein grosses farbiges und sehr gut beleuchtetes Element befindet.

208

RESORTING TO GRAY far from being boring can be an i
alternative to get a much more intimate atmosphere with r
subdued lighting. Topcounter washbasins can enhance
brightness and presence beautifying the environment just
chrome accessories.

RECURRIR AL GRIS lejos de ser aburrido puede ser una altern
ideal para obtener una atmósfera mucho más íntima con
nación más tenue. Los lavabos de sobreponer pueden ace
su brillo y presencia embelleciendo el ambiente al igual qu
accesorios cromados.

LE GRIS, loin d'être ennuyeux, peut devenir une alternative i
pour obtenir une ambiance beaucoup plus intime avec un éclo
plus doux. Les lavabos à superposer peuvent accentuer leur
et leur présence, en embellissant l'ambiance, de même q
accessoires chromés.

AUF GRAU ZURÜCKZUGREIFEN, kann, weit davon e
langweilig zu sein, eine ideale Alternative sein, um eine se
privatere Atmosphäre mit einer sanfteren Beleuchtung zu sch
Der Glanz und die Präsenz der aufgesetzen Waschbecke
betont und sie verschönern, wie auch das verchromte Zu
das Ambiente.

modern
moderno
moderne
modern

Warm and always cozy the bathroom should convey serenity and calm. The elegance of the lines, care in materials, attention to detail and personalization through textures or controlled luminous scenes are essential.

Cálido y siempre acogedor el cuarto de baño debe trasmitir serenidad y calma. La elegancia de las líneas, el cuidado en los materiales, la atención al detalle y la personalización a través de texturas o escenas lumínicas controladas son esenciales.

La salle de bain, toujours accueillante, doit transmettre sérénité et calme. L'élégance des lignes, le soin des matériaux, l'attention prêtée à chaque détail, ainsi que la personnalisation à travers des textures y des scènes de lumière contrôlées, sont essentielles.

Warm und immer gemütlich sollte das Badezimmer Gelassenheit und Ruhe vermitteln. Die Eleganz der Linien, die sorgfältig gewählten Materialien, die Aufmerksamkeit bei den Details und die persönliche Note durch Texturen oder kontrollierte Lichtinszenierungen sind essentiell.

Light and colors are closely linked, that's why to choose a certain color will depend on the type of lighting the environment has, either day or night. For a more closed space warm light works, on the contrary a space with natural lighting will need cold light.

La luz y los colores están estrechamente vinculados, por lo que escoger un color determinado dependerá del tipo de iluminación con la que cuente el ambiente, ya sea de día o de noche. Para un espacio más cerrado la luz cálida funciona, por el contrario, un espacio con iluminación natural necesitará luz fría.

La lumière et les couleurs sont étroitement liées, donc, le choix d'une certaine couleur dépendra du type d'éclairage de l'ambian que ce soit de jour ou de nuit. Pour un espace plus fermé, la lumière chaude fonctionne, tandis que, pour un espace ayant un éclairage naturel, il faudra une lumière froide.

Licht und Farben sind direkt miteinander verknüpft, darum hängt die Wahl einer bestimmten Farbe von der Art Beleuchtung ab, die es im Ambiente gibt, sei es am Tag oder in der Nacht. Für einen eher geschlossenen Bereich ist warmes Licht angemessen, im Gegenteil benötigt ein Bereich mit natürlichem Licht eher eine kalte Beleuchtu

When interior design incorporates several variations of tones and materials, we can use simple lines of furniture for not saturating the space visually. Not counting with decorative elements is ideal if the space is small but if the area is more spacious we can use comfortable armchairs with discreet appearance that allow the delight to observe when taking a short break.

Cuando el diseño interior incorpora diversas variaciones de tonos y materiales puede recurrirse a mobiliario de trazos sencillos para no saturar visualmente el espacio. Prescindir de elementos decorativos es idóneo si el espacio es pequeño pero si el área es más amplia se puede recurrir a confortables sillones de apariencia discreta que permitan el deleite de observar al tomar un breve descanso.

Quand le design d'intérieur incorpore diverses variations de tons et matériaux, on peut utiliser un mobilier aux traits simples pour ne pas saturer visuellement l'espace. Se passer d'éléments de décoration est parfait quand l'espace est petit, mais si la surface est plus grande, on peut utiliser des fauteuils confortables d'apparence discrète, qui permettent le plaisir d'observer en prenant un moment de repos.

Wenn die Innendekoration aus verschiedensten Tönen und Materialien besteht, sollte auf Möbel mit schlichten Linien zurückgegriffen werden, um den Bereich nicht optisch zu übersättigen. Auf dekorative Elemente zu verzichten ist ideal wenn der Bereich klein ist, aber wenn der Raum grösser ist, kann man bequeme, diskrete Sessel wählen, die es erlauben die Aussicht zu geniessen, während man sich kurz ausruht.

TO ACHIEVE A MODERN LOOK we can select furniture with simple and straight lines, without moldings, without marked streaks, without upholstery pattern, just plain colors. All this in a sober space in which we can incorporate a work of art or a designer's lighting fixture will be the ideal complement for your space.

PARA LOGRAR UN AIRE MODERNO puede seleccionarse mobiliario de líneas simples y rectas, sin molduras, sin vetas marcadas, sin tapizados estampados, simplemente colores lisos. Todo ello en conjunto con un espacio sobrio al cual se podrá incorporar una obra de arte o alguna luminaria de diseñador serán el complemento ideal para tu espacio.

POUR RÉUSSIR UN AIR MODERNE, on peut choisir un mobilier aux lignes simples et droites, sans moulures, sans veines marquées, sans tapisseries imprimées, seulement des couleurs lisses. Tout cela sera uni à un espace sobre auquel on pourra incorporer une œuvre d'art ou une lampe design, qui seront le complément idéal de cet espace.

UM EIN MODERNES AUSSEHEN zu erzielen kann man Möbel mit einfacher, gerader Linienführung wählen, ohne Verzierungen, ohne deutliche Maserung, ohne gemusterte Polster, schlicht einfarbig. All dies in einem nüchternen Bereich, zu dem man ein Kunstwerk oder eine Designerleuchte hinzufügen kann, die ideale Ergänzungen für diesen Bereich sind.

IT'S A MYTH THAT WARM AND COLD SHOULD NOT BE MERGED. The combination works but it needs to be done o
the walls can match with the bathroom accessories and the chrome taps while furniture do the same with decorative piece
key is to properly define the color temperature taking into account the tones that dominate the space the most.

ES UN MITO QUE LO CÁLIDO Y LO FRÍO NO DEBAN FUSIONARSE. La combinación funciona pero habrá que h
ordenadamente: a los muros les puede corresponder dialogar con los accesorios de baño y la grifería cromada mientr
a los muebles hacen lo propio con piezas decorativas. La clave es definir adecuadamente la temperatura de color tor
en cuenta los tonos que dominen más el espacio.

UN MYTHE QUE L'ON NE PUISSE PAS FUSIONNER LE CHAUD ET LE FROID. La combinaison fonctionne, mais il la faire de façon ordonnée: les murs doivent dialoguer avec les accessoires de bain et la robinetterie chromée, tandis s meubles doivent le faire avec les pièces décoratives. La clé est de définir comme il faut la température de la couleur es tons qui dominent sur l'espace.

WARM UND KALT NICHT MITEINANDER KOMBINIERT WERDEN SOLLTEN IST EIN MYTHOS. Die Kombination niert gut, aber man muss es in einer geordneten Weise machen: die Wände können mit dem Badezimmerzubehör und maturen in Dialog stehen, während die Möbel das Gleiche mit den dekorativen Stücken machen. Der Trick besteht darin peratur der Farbe, die dominanten Töne im Bereich berücksichtigend, angemessen zu definieren.

Selecting a bathtub with a vintage touch will allow you to turn it into
the protagonist of the space and therefore it will define the range and
tone of colors that can be used. A translucent curtain can provide a
level of comfort and pleasant lighting.

Seleccionar una tina de baño con un toque *vintage* te permitirá
convertirla en la protagonista del espacio y en consecuencia
definirá la gama de colores y acentos que se prodrán emplear.
Una cortina traslúcida puede brindar un nivel de iluminación
confortable y ameno.

Choisir une baignoire avec une touche *vintage* permettra de
la transformer en protagoniste de l'espace, et c'est elle qui, en
conséquence, définira la gamme de couleurs et accents à utiliser.
Un rideau translucide permet d'apporter un niveau d'éclairage
confortable et agréable.

Eine Badewanne im *Vintage* Stil wird zum Protagonist im Bereich
und definiert folglich die Farbpalette und die Akzente, die gesetzt
werden können. Ein lichtdurchlässiger Vorhang erlaubt eine
angemessene und angenehme Beleuchtung.

RIBUTION WILL ALWAYS BE IMPORTANT to perceive and our spaces harmoniously. In small places, we should be ful not to include furniture that can disturb or reduce circulation s. In larger spaces, relying on the presence of a small garden ncrease the desirable level of relaxation and comfort. Do not t that a bathroom is a intimate meeting point with comfort.

STRIBUCIÓN SIEMPRE SERÁ IMPORTANTE para percibir plear armónicamente nuestros espacios. En lugares eños se debe ser prudente de no incluir muebles que puedan nodar o reducir las zonas de circulación. En espacios más os recurrir a la presencia de un pequeño jardín permite incre-r el nivel de relajación y comodidad deseable. No hay lvidar que un cuarto de baño es un punto de encuentro con la comodidad.

LA DISTRIBUTION SERA TOUJOURS IMPORTANTE pour percevoir et utiliser harmonieusement nos espaces. Dans les petits espaces, il est prudent de ne pas inclure des meubles qui puissent gêner ou réduire les zones de circulation. Dans les espaces plus amples, un petit jardin permet d'augmenter le niveau de détente et confort que l'on désire. Il ne faut pas oublier qu'une salle de bain est un point de rencontre intime avec le confort.

DIE ANORDNUNG IST IMMER WICHTIG, um unsere Räume harmonisch zu empfinden und zu nutzen. In kleinen Bereichen sollte man so umsichtig sein, keine Möbel zu verwenden, die behindern oder die Bewegungsfreiheit einengen. In grösseren Räumen erlaubt ein kleiner Garten das Niveau der Entspannung und gewünschter Annehmlichkeit zu erhöhen. Man darf nicht vergessen, dass ein Badezimmer ein Ort des intimen Zusammentreffens mit Behaglichkeit ist.

rustic
rústico
rustique
rustikal

IN RUSTIC STYLE DOMINATES THE ORGANIC, free forms of nature and everything that seems to speak of time and life, everything that has marks, cracks, textures or colors. Therefore, to decorate with very colorful seasonal elements gives vitality and distinction to each element of architectural design. It makes a space unique, a space that can take us to our childhood or to certain known places. The rustic is a space voyage to the comfort of the past.

EN EL ESTILO RÚSTICO DOMINA LO ORGÁNICO, las formas libres de la naturaleza y todo aquello que parece hablarnos del tiempo y la vida, lo que posee marcas, las grietas, las texturas o los colores. Por todo ello, decorar con elementos estacionales muy coloridos da vitalidad y distinción a cada elemento de diseño arquitectónico; convierte en único un espacio que puede trasladarnos a nuestra infancia o a ciertos lugares conocidos. Lo rústico es un viaje espacial hacia la comodidad del pasado.

LE STYLE RUSTIQUE est dominé par ce qui est organique, les formes libres de la nature et tout ce qui paraît nous parler du temps et de la vie, ce qui possède des marques, les fissures, les textures ou les couleurs. C'est pour cela que décorer avec des éléments de la saison pleins de couleur donne de la vitalité et de la distinction à chaque élément de design architectural, transforme en quelque chose d'unique un espace qui peut nous ramener à notre enfance ou à certains endroits familiers. Le rustique est un voyage spatial vers le confort du passé.

IM RUSTIKALEN STIL herrscht das Organische vor, die freien Formen der Natur und alles was uns über die Zeit und das Leben zu erzählen scheint, was gezeichnet ist, Risse, Texturen oder Farben. Daher bietet die Dekoration mit farbenfrohen jahreszeitlichen Elementen, Lebendigkeit und etwas Besonderes in jedem architektonischen Design; verwandelt einen Bereich in etwas Einzigartiges, das uns in unsere Kindheit oder an vergangene Orte versetzt. Der rustikale Stil ist eine Reise in die Annehmlichkeiten der Vergangenheit.

oresence of stone elements in light or dark tones is definitely
led. They are a hallmark of the construction details that well
uted they turn into something more than decoration when
mpanied by sculptures or flower arrangements in a small size.

esencia de elementos pétreos en tonos claros u oscuros no
e faltar, son un sello distintivo de los detalles constructivos que
bien ejecutados se convierten en algo más que en decoración
do se acompañan de piezas escultóricas o arreglos florales
equeño formato.

La présence d'éléments de pierre aux tons clairs ou foncés ne doit
pas manquer, étant un sceau distinctif des détails de construction qui,
très bien exécutés, deviennent quelque chose de plus qu'une simple
décoration, quand ils s'accompagnent de sculptures ou de bouquets
à petit format.

Elemente aus Stein in hellen oder dunklen Farben sollten nicht
fehlen; sie sind der besondere Akzent in den baulichen Details,
die, wenn sie gut gearbeitet sind und von Skulpturen oder kleinen
Blumenarrangements begleitet werden, mehr sind als nur Dekoration.

architecture arquitectónicos architectoniques architekten

19 *architectural and interior design project:* S+DISEÑO sara tamez

20 *architectural project:* ABAX, fernando de haro l., jesús fernández., omar fuentes e., bertha figueroa p.

24-125 *architectural project:* RDLP ARQUITECTOS, rodrigo de la peña

30-131 *architectural project:* AGRAZ ARQUITECTOS, ricardo agraz

32-133 *architectural project:* BRACHET PROJECT MANAGEMENT, yvan brachet

34 *architectural project:* PGM ARQUITECTURA, patricio garcía m.

36 *architectural project and interior design project:* GRUPO MM

37 *architectural project:* PASCAL ARQUITECTOS, carlos pascal, gerard pascal

38-139 *architectural project:* AGRAZ ARQUITECTOS, ricardo agraz

41 *architectural project:* MURO ROJO ARQUITECTURA, elizabeth gómez c., jorge medina

42-143 *architectural project and interior design project:* GRUPO MM

44-145 *architectural project:* ARCO arquitectura contemporánea, josé lew k., bernardo lew k.

46 *architectural project:* BRACHET PROJECT MANAGEMENT, yvan brachet

48 *architectural project:* AGRAZ ARQUITECTOS, ricardo agraz

49 *architectural project:* DIM INGENIEROS Y ARQUITECTOS, carlos dayan, eduardo dayan, enrique levy o.

50 *architectural project:* ARQUIPLAN, bernardo hinojosa m.

51 *architectural project:* SERRANO MONJARAZ ARQUITECTOS, juan pablo serrano o., rafael monjaraz f.

R Zero, edgar velasco / *interior design project:* isabel maldonado

52-153 *architectural project:* LÓPEZ DUPLAN ARQUITECTOS, claudia lópez duplan

54-155 *architectural project:* REIMS ARQUITECTURA, eduardo reims h., jorge reims h.

56-157 *architectural and interior design project:* GA GRUPO ARQUITECTURA, daniel álvarez f.

58-159 *architectural project:* ULISES CASTAÑEDA ARQUITECTOS, ulises castañeda s.

62-163 *architectural project:* ABAX, fernando de haro l., jesús fernández s., omar fuentes e., bertha figueroa p.

64-165 *architectural and interior design project:* A CREATIVE PROCESS, andrés saavedra

66-167 *architectural and interior design project:* 2E ARTE VISUAL, juan carlos doce

? *architectural project:* GRUPO ARQUITECTÓNICA, genaro nieto i.

0-171 *architectural project:* LUISER GÓMEZ ARQUITECTO, luis ernesto gómez

2-173 *architectural project:* ABAX, fernando de haro l., jesús fernández., omar fuentes e., bertha figueroa p.

4 *interior design project:* CDS C-CHIC DESIGN STUDIO, olga mussali h., sara mizrahi e.

75-177 *interior design project:* CDS C-CHIC DESIGN STUDIO, olga mussali h., sara mizrahi e.

8 *architectural project:* ARQUIPLAN, bernardo hinojosa m.

9 *architectural and interior design project:* EXTRACTO arte, arquitectura y diseño, vanessa patiño, robert duarte

0-181 *architectural project:* MURO ROJO ARQUITECTURA, elizabeth gómez c., jorge medina

2-183 *architectural project:* a.a.a ALMAZÁN ARQUITECTOS Y ASOCIADOS, guillermo almazán c.,

llermo suárez a., dirk thurmer f.

architecture arquitectónicos architectoniques architekter